I0163664

A SPANISH GALLEON

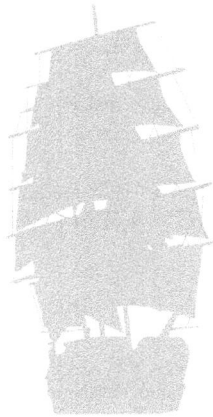

David-Joseph François Brière

Copyright © 2016 David-Joseph François Brière.

David-Joseph François Brière
4340 Kaslo St. Vancouver, BC V5R2B7
865-323-6601
David-Joseph François Brière

All rights reserved. No part of this book may be reproduced, stored, or transmitted by any means–whether auditory, graphic, mechanical, or electronic–without written permission of both publisher and author, except in the case of brief excerpts used in critical articles and reviews. Unauthorized reproduction of any part of this work is illegal and is punishable by law.

ISBN: 978-0-578-18341-1 (sc)
ISBN: 978-0-578-18342-8 (e)

Because of the dynamic nature of the Internet, any web addresses or links contained in this book may have changed since publication and may no longer be valid. The views expressed in this work are solely those of the author and do not necessarily reflect the views of the publisher, and the publisher hereby disclaims any responsibility for them.

Any people depicted in stock imagery provided by Thinkstock are models, and such images are being used for illustrative purposes only.
Certain stock imagery © Thinkstock.

Lulu Publishing Services rev. date: 11/18/2016

ARMADA

Armada
Politician of the sea
I want to hear your creaking doctrine.
Your ropes, war tassels
Your mast, unconquerable in ardor
Slash the emerald currents with your lunging stem,
and teach us your language of ease.
Our allegiance to you, Armada
Unfathomable

FLORIDA MORASS

Florida Morass, untamable land
Sporadic in its discord, intestine
Hatching age-old hoary specimens, privy in the undergrowth.
Fish cave decay
Carom back to the boa tongue
and cry your mate summon
in hollow bark reverb
Star-rouse
Ancient monolith rising from the oil
Screech muted to a vacant vacuum totem.

VOICE INFLECTION

Voice Inflection
The sounds are starting guns
Long distance runners find groves

BELTANE

Monstrous, fervent embers bleed
to the ardent superstition.
Wherefore the lamb slain?
Wild Sabbatical release.
Strive!
Full chalice accord.
To swards we lean devotion.

CREEK THAW

A second, one second
Thawing creek revisited
That lonely blue frost again and again
Rare war medals in his palm.
Awe
"I can't believe the terror back there."

SNAKESKIN HUT

Snakeskin Hut mystery
       Reptile egg crackle-vein
Hearts of the forest connected
       Electro-web artery
Warrior-hunters pulling ropes in red unison
Turn a blind eye know-it-all-don't-move-your-head-keep-walking
       The furious ambush
Jaguar in heat
       moss follow sun blood ruche
A bible exchanges hands,
       in a swamp.

GRAIN ASSEMBLY

Lo, the fortune's echo,
dismal, its impulse.
Laconic exclusion
Rising tide.

Still, restive grain
in prorogued swarm.
emergence to assignment
Brume-cast translations

Under the lesion, refer.
Anodyne polyp, recede.
Prone to rancor
Sustain!

Bovine, bract-less. Broad bevy brusquely behaved.
Surge sanction afore dour conceit.

THERE WAS BARELY ANY TIME

The buildings were sinking so quickly into the hill,
There was barely time for jail

And when the river, at length, told us its final vow
And we look'd out far,
And saw our sure end, fated

Well, you can rest assured,
We were already on our way home.

SNAKE CRUCIFIXION

Our most difficult concern came in August
When the snake hung bleeding from the time tree.
One charred offering to the living God.
Crude mouth gasping
and golden stomach moaning frail reproach
      A young boy drowns in tears.
"Cold."
Anatomy Lesson for children.
Holy persuasion of Sunday.
    The slow organ mused.
Piano abandoned, overgrown with vines
There's an intermission at the town play.
      Tuning fork to girl punishment
Sun Stroke necessity and
Impatient revelry for a morrow hour
whiskey haven that never comes.
Last inquisition.
      A mystic is missing
      The slaughter has finished
      Fascination dispelled
Eyes now content
Walk up wooden stairs
Clack
Clack

Clack
Clack
looking side to side in a windowsill
Shifting to intangibile duress.
      Voyeur
Fantasy duchess-face statue
Rises
Sun yolk'd settlement awake
The servants have come
Bearing smiles
With holy gifts
to endure the slow extinction.

TWO JACKALS

Two Jackals stick their head out of the car
and begin talking.
"Hehe hehe haha haha hehe"
Their green faces move.
Each horrible second is a torturous power struggle.
"Yeah, alright, see ya"
They ride off in cacophonous laughter,
looking for someone new to use and kill.
How has God made this?
How can I play nicely in this wanton, broken land of thieves?

A SPANISH GALLEON

A Spanish Galleon
Cuts like a javelin
Everything else - falls

NIGHTS OF YOUTH

Nights of youth
First encounters
Sex on a deserted beach
Cool wind and warm skin
and the stingray cosmos
Wild nights of youth
Time

INDIANS IN SNOW

Indians in snow
Distant orange glow
Under wild skins,
The blue continent sleeps

FARRAGUT

Cicada song
Belvedere char hill
Horses dying
in a stale, sun-sickened shed.

"Their ain't no meat on them bones."
Fuel for afternoon stare-contest.
Vacuum vacancy.

Poor sad jester, head in his hands
Doesn't like seeing pain.
"Was that you over there?"

The elderly tried to save the high school
but it burned down, down, down, down to the ground.

Postcard from the tropics.

An end to thralldom display
And swift return to Martyrdom.
Proprietors of our own estates,
We act as we please
Sinking in comfort.

Feel the suburban sprinklers in the night.
Wild nude rambling downhill
Plunging valley.
Wet pines.
Buried arrows.
"Let me see your gun collection."
         "-I thought you'd never ask."

YOUNG WITCHES

Young witches, jocund,
dance naked on the fringes of town,
     projecting wild, fervent visions while the mayor sleeps.
I think you've seen this one before,
     in your living room.

A SMALL BAND OF ADOLESCENTS

A small band of adolescents
walk through the hallways of an abandoned building,
smashing out lights and knocking over chairs.
The dead stand in silence watching and shrug.

HER HEART WAS

Her heart was
A wooded path
Uphill and sunlit
in vivid elysian dawn
Nursing doe,
To the undying grove.
A fortress
secret from the province
Ages

EXILE

I remember my old life before I deserted it
The vigorous machines
Words
and those eager ones,
Screaming, screeching, and jousting at the sun in a fury.
Now I am a strange animal on the empty shores,
examining loose debris.
All shells and mollusks are there stimulating my fascination.
Salty pools stretch the land without end.
Hell is just proposal in vast, ocean exile.

THE KING'S GRAVE

It rained at the King's grave
His epitaph had faded
This was years ago.

SKYLARK

Skylark wat'ry waving herald
Rouse the estranged
Plovers planted, mute
We hail thee

Fenced in dissent
Useless pleated denouncing
Plead to the jowl
Flouted impressions

Assembly o'er truest hue
inauguration held
Gifts from the woodland
Word to the winds
Deter the invidious
Imponderable strath foresight devour

YOU CANNOT ESCAPE

Tea is brewed
and beauty flourishes.
A tough concept for
Brokers, policemen, pharmacists, radio hosts, fast food employees
& gun salesman.
You cannot escape!

NOTE ON FILM

Film is the fervent pinnacle of man.
The yearning toil of the human psyche,
unconsciously, since its primal beginnings.
A desire to escape into an identical world.
The last century is simply a product of boredom.

ASYLUM

Asylum
Girl in white gown running through the night
headlights behind her
     -bad trip
Black bulbous oil
     -the devil
"She's made a lot of progress, sir."
Rife ammonia scent and bad lighting
"State"
The county commissioner is adulterous
Gears grinding
Iron towers
     chain gang
Curious eyes roll down the window
     (Ravenous engine hum)
"Let me give you a ride"
Dropping the knife
Trembling in terror
Barefoot in the road

I AM THE GHOST MAN

I am the Ghost Man
of the wayward chateau.
I drift the hallways,
aborted to all,
recollecting the endless scene I witnessed
alone in the upstairs bedroom.
I laid on the bed,
the door
sternly closed,
handle turning,
seemingly on its own.
And it was not the wind, oh, no, no, no.
Now I await my divine trial,
sitting by a candle,
dejected and staring,
while outside, a battle rages
and the new measuring stick is procured
to measure my penis.
Notice of eviction.
I cannot wait
for tomorrow morning.

MEDIEVAL SWELL

Pilfered and pinioned
Reverie's one last stand.
Stragglers of sun,
Converse amongst yourselves.

Lordship enthroned,
Inrush'd patience.
The castle breathes
and all simply falls into place.

Drawers opened,
Searched time,
communication is abounding
charter'd occurrence.

Lush wilderness freed
Miracles happening here on earth at this very moment.

SLIDING DOORS

Beggar in town, forgotten.
Dying in the hot, arid summer.
Man leaves office,
Passing him on the way back to his quaint home.
Dinner is served.
The two will never meet.

STAKE YOUR CLAIM

Stake fast, your claim.
"Can you believe how big our tree has gotten?"
      One syllable and your at my throat.
Take your things and go
There are plenty of hollows left
to mock you.

BLACK MAN IN A SUIT

Black man in a suit
anomaly forever, probably
Sad notion for a guy who gets outta bed each day
Don't be so afraid, he's come to celebrate

"Can't tell you what
Cuz I don't know
I Can't get mad
Ain't got no foe
Little darlin"

The river man is down there
Tell your troubles and he will find you a ring in the mud

Somebody jump off this massive cliff, here
Ah, I knew you'd do it ya sly dog you

Down river we float, reveling in our will, and watching as a man
walks along
with a gentle, tired, unchained, ethereal, sun-soaked grin.
A wild canyon freed.

Overhead flight plan
Travel on, travel on, travel on, travel on, travel on

HIGH NOON ATROPHY

High noon atrophy
Farmers planting sugarcane
　　Squinting up the road

BOYNTON BEACH

Aztec Migration
All abandoned tombs and artifacts
Make for a one-track-mind.

Cacophonous Serum Rig.
New venom is discovered.
Martyr marrow mound
Turning in absentee ballots this year.

Snake Rattle in the humid morning,
All rise.

"Have you come here to confess?
Her fate is in your hands, sir."
    Stained Oak & ornate, overlooked carvings
-"Yes, yes, all of this, yes"
    "Please help"
    Skyward glances into the overcast.

Embrace the uncertainty.
Ignore these dumb beasts.

An orchestra playing and child running with a flag
"Please be seated, this is an important, emotive piece."

"Bellicose"

The casino, soaked in bourbon
Joyous in its lavish deferment.
Eager and separate from the green glow of interstate.
Serving city with soul
Elegance

Bitter end to the humble; Roman Rule
        Revolution on the playground tether

Akashic Radio
All actions on cassette tape for personal enjoyment
"I see what you did there"
        Angels singing

The bullet enters the rifle, and its gunman observes himself
observing himself
A simple need for gentleman's clubs

A la muerte
Magellan hit with a poisoned arrow in the Pacific Isles
and an absent fleet
Engraved emulsion in Eden
Beautiful garden
Fenced in.

THE MAIDS

The Maids did not have to clean.

RUSSIAN HEIRESS

"I don't care where ya go, you can't sleep here"
Fame drives change for pleasant regulars
25 cents gets you a friendly glance
"I'm glad you guys are friends, so we can all have a thanksgiving dinner together."

Russian Heiress, I am captive to your hysteria
Cackling for all to hear
Yes, you are a league apart, it is true.
Louder now, for they all seek your madness.

(We then see a man seduced on the way out, he is surprised but quite receptive.)

The cool slip of brume-night air
Releases
and is giving
and keeps those deserving few in favorable deliverance.

If I get rich, you won't receive a dime.

SUBMARINE FEAR

Submarine fear
Armageddon
Looking for a cave fish to eat us.

HOW CAN I EXPLAIN

My words mean nothing because of Our Savior.

The mysterious powers of Sage
driving out all wickedness on Earth.

How can I explain
What is purposely hidden?

STILL

I move
        -he coughs
The game of not moving.

PARKED UPON THE HILL

Drinking in my car
City lights burning below
The war still withstood

END OF DAYS

Their intelligence, much like a matador
Sharp lunges into uncertainty.

Photograph of a young, naked woman
The local papers

I give my friend a shipwrecked Spanish coin
from out of the sea.
He says he is going to attach it to his balls
and tell those curious, inquisitive souls that it was in fact, I, who
gave him the coin.

Ha

The Book of Solomon
End of Days

The dead summer park catches fire.
Cop goes home and drinks himself to babble.

A salute to this vulgar wreck of shit.

1965 FORMAL

A banner, swaying.
1965 Formal
Mary Ann, undressed.

TREEHOUSE

An old treehouse hangs sullen and abandoned in a woods
as we approach and gaze.

SITTING FROM THE HOTEL CHAIR

I stare at the mirror
from the hotel chair,
waiting for the bedside lamp to fly into it.
I've heard of this before
And as the time goes on,
My concern does only grow.
      Thick fog in the jungle night
Do your thing
See you soon.

DEFERRED

Bitter precepts close
Preface to quick desertion
Revolution hides in watches

Slow, slender hands pull back red curtains
and reveal garbage
strewed all over the floor

What a Relief
"For your sake, we hope you like convulsions"
Talk plague
Oil in the glass
Nice ass
"Don't even think of moving too fast"

Broomstick in the spokes
Good time

SPINAL FLUID

Rusty commune, ruins against knife's edge
Cliff hanger night to a running engine
And without delay, you can rest assured.
Hollow morning.
"Well, you know, we all have our dead dog days."
A new creed, formed in the house.
The orgy in the shed is finished.
Sudden, nauseous qualm
"Band of the Backwoods"
An old flag hangs tattered in the window.
Conceived too late against the psychic grid.
Scrapyard Man postures with his cigarette,
as his legs barely hold his creaky frame.
"Like Butch Cassidy and the Sundance Kid!"
A dirty dog trots in from the side, panting as the sun beats down.
True patriot.
Trepidation on the hillside.
A western gun fight just right up the road.
"Drive safe."

FREEWAY

The wheels on the freeway speak
fear at night
undercarriage thin in withered gallop
strain in the currents
Meeting the eyes of a wolf on the bank
Tumbleweed & chains
Teeth chattering
A wind-up toy cartoon
Acid armpit sweat trickle almost there
The calm, groaning presence of heat lightning
Frail and rusted barbed wire
"Where are we?"
The banshee-crone with her town Revival
Hitting our shins as she walks with her cane
Is certainly no end resolution
Nor her deluging
I laid down and my head
dissolved in the bone-dry grinding of Western expansion.

MIRAGE

      Mirage in the parking lot
What are we to do
      but keep on walking

BELL TOWER

A lighthouse devoured by a wave
       Reverence to the living.
I stay in the bellower,
Keeping record of the Vedas.
A phantom citadel bordering the sea.
       Is the silence too great?
The wind is cold iron to the ear.
The blue night is giving moan.
       Give space to the dying
Today marks the birth of when the ocean bespoke.

OUTER REACHES

Seek
North America - 600 year impulse
Qualified, certain. (Byzantine)
Wooden bridges over water
And quantitative reasoning still triumphs, yes.
Danger before revision
Then sinister word traps before elders
      -don't get caught
Religious authority is becoming humane as a result of innate purge
Change
Might as well never sit down.
The old ways are crumbl'ing every second passed.
Someone invents the suit.
"This is the way, my friend."
      -"Ain't seen a guy do it like him…"
Poetry can't really reinvent
But then again
What ever could
Besides
      Trust
Where is our alternative earth?
The rent is due
and for miles, the swift sea.

There's a knock at the door
          "Have a good time in jail!"
Well that's quite the claim.
"I never touched her!"
          Plane crash
A guide walks us through a maze of atrocities after death.
God
What's new?
To carry one thought for a lifetime.
          "Never mind those disgusting, putrid beggars"
When you stand informing them of the dog's breed,
prepare to be vastly mistaken.
A sweaty rental shop owner closes up
and goes home holding a crucifix.
          -"A little too close to call, I think. You might not be as good
as you think you are."
Morning magick
mending burn holes in the film screen.
He quickly sells a radio.
Moving mouths go silent.
A train yard
Twitching in the night.
I drove into the sun.
This evening has been very much appreciated.
May I leave the table?

ABOUT THE AUTHOR

David-Joseph François Brière attended and graduated from the Vancouver Film School. He is a writer and filmmaker currently living in Vancouver, British Columbia.

www.ingramcontent.com/pod-product-compliance
Lightning Source LLC
Chambersburg PA
CBHW060618030426
42337CB00018B/3100